A Kind of Tide

© 2008 by Carl Norman

The poems "In Earnest" and "Two" first appeared in the Fall 2002 issue of *The Northwoods Journal*.

ISBN: 1-4392-1938-9

For my mother, forever;
for the Princess, just as well.

Sincere gratitude to
Chris, Amanda, and Normalynn,
without whom none of this
would have been possible.

Contents

I. Vacant Treehouse

II. Etiquette's Long Faces

III. Naked Crayons

IV. The Dove

V. Myths & Legends

VI. Chimera

I

Vacant Treehouse

"He who sits alone, rests alone,
walks alone unindolent,
who in solitude controls himself,
will find delight in the forest."

The Dhammapada

In Earnest

I walk a crooked path in life.
My steps are staggered and untrue.
I walk alone, Fate in my hands.
I trace my tears, where they might go.

I am not often led astray,
For it is my own course I chart.
There is no map to mark the way
Save the atlas of my heart.

In all great failure, all great loss,
I have always stood alone;
Sought wisdom in sorrow, patience in woe;
Steadfast friends I have not known.

I do not hide behind my past.
Nor spurn the lessons of trials before.
I've walked the long road as both young and young fool,
Thus am bound to neither anymore.

I shall always walk alone.
Though age, though time might wear me down.
I fear not what might lie ahead;
Where I've been's worse than where I'm bound.

In leaving the womb I learned to cry.
Alone since then, I've not been dry.
Yet proud hold I my head up high;
As I was born, so shall I die.

The Gunslinger

The young man walked in to the bar
trying to not be grim
but aware Woe's vile subtleties
adore such smoky din.

His eyes, alert, were fortunate
to spy a candles glare
as it crossed the table where his past was.
She had been long waiting for him there.

(Way back when he'd sent her off
he had not realized the costs.
For often today things termed forsaken
we ruefully tomorrow define as loss.)

He stood still in lieu of running as
she had not seen him yet.
Though Prudence ought wisely take to foot
in the face of past's regret.

And when she turned and saw his face
he did not flee, but smiled instead.
She returned the smile, then rose, then left,
leaving him for dead.

California

―――――――――

I came upon the wreckage by accident
as often is the case with these things
having detoured my way
to this place in time. Perhaps they did too.
We all have our trials.

A lumpy tarp lay beside the road
covering someone's tragedy
everyone's tragedy
and it seemed so impossibly small, frail,
that lump in the center of it
like a tiny bird egg in the palm of a large hand.
I wondered where that life force went
as it vibrated away to a different plateau
either faster or slower, than I
perhaps to a place of quiet, of bliss.
Perhaps even to nowhere, or everywhere.

I stood, transfixed,
drown in the tide of a tear
as if one hundred generations
of emotional poverty
were suddenly being rinsed out, washed away
by the death of a child.

I turned away misty
to scan the distant tree line for a Redwood
with that timeless wisdom, eternal silence;
branches spread like the far-flung beauty
of a child's laughing eyes.
I remember when they used to live
in this part of California.

If

If I died would you come to my funeral?
Would you care to shed a tear?
Could you let your heart cry out for me
once I'm no longer here?

As the pastor spoke his calming words
and it's clear I've no tomorrow,
would you wear a long, black veil
to hide your face's sorrow?

When the silent few who mourn are gone
and I'm lowered in the ground
would you regret the time we missed
while I was still around?

Would photos boxed in a dusty attic
that you barely chose to save
find their place upon your mantle
were my body in the grave?

No words console a mourning soul;
No songs replace joys lost;
Pride fills all forecasts of demise
once we neglect life's costs.

Don't let the breath of life be gone
before you choose to care.
Don't leave me here, alone, alive
while you live lonely there.

Dawn

This could be the place
where a reel change flickers
a skittish white frame
across the screen of life.

It could be the final paragraph
of another wordy chapter
though early enough in the story
that reading it, spine stretched on a pillow,
mulling it over a time or two
isn't such a hard thing to do.

It could be the beginning of a cocoon's separation
an egg's cracking, a wave's breaking,
even a star's death.

It could be spring.

for Dale, that she not despair

The Princess

———————

I saw you one day in a Laundromat
with a passel of ornery children at your feet
each wanting to be your jester.
The worn silk scarf adorning
your True Auburn Highlights
looks like a golden crown to me
and I assume you have a newer one
less frayed, less tattered, less tight
in the warm, soft treasury
that is your laundry basket.
And your troops, in dress formation
stand before you in proper rows
like so many metal sentinels
always willing to serve to the death
in hot, warm, or cold
for a coin or two, and your touch.
I see the hope
in the shades of your sweat
and the hope eternal
of tomorrow in your eyes
The hope that is your courtier
and never far away
from the life you live,
and the lint that makes you sneeze
and is static-stuck to your faded blouse
like a wash-n-wear war ribbon
won from the battle of despair.
And in the eternal struggle deemed life
you are beautiful...

A Rainbow

All of my young life I've sought
The pot that I was told
Was at the end of rainbows
And filled with precious gold.

I traveled many different ways
Searching both far and wide.
Yet saw no rainbow, saw no pot
Saw no gold inside.

Eventually my searched ended
For desire is wont to stall.
I had found no rainbow, found no pot,
Found no gold at all

Then one fine day I met a girl
With rainbows in her eyes.
And in her heart, the pot of gold
Which she gave me as a prize.

For long I thought my rainbow
Was late or overdue
But good things come to those who wait
As I've found my gold in you.

Hiwis '42

The rats, the rats, were trying
to hide like an old woman
in a dark, dank Stalingrad basement
as a Panzer growls by, prowls by,
rumbles along in a casual way
barrel blazing sun-like and all-seeing
evil, even,
probing through broken walls, floors, promises
for her alone
matriarch of the dead city.

The Attic

Glistening tears of a bygone age
Burst forth today as a bitter rage.
Since advice from a fool, heard as words of a sage
Have landed a bird in a gilded cage

From this attic I watch the world.

They loosed and fluffed their silken tresses
As I wallowed in a convict's mires.
And they swayed within fine summer dresses
Like bells within a church's spires.
They sang of the love, so gaily written
That as virgin youths they longed to know.
As I was with loneliness smitten
They romped in grace on a picture show

Plastic painted faces aglow.

Avarice gathers in these silty eaves.
Broken glass cuts the rain-swept breeze.
The shutters bang and the rafters wheeze,
While the body drops to tattered knees

Likely to deceive.

Forsaken long within this world
I shall not cry the sorrow's tear.
As if the ranks of men were such:
Possessed of joys that I might share

For all the brothers in lockdown

The Dance

Sing a bossa nova to the sky inside
emptiness in shades of blue
(rising to black
rising to black)
that someone gave a name to
and the rest just go along with it to
Keep Hope Alive.

Cotton candy clouds
shoo away the butterflies
dethroned Monarch's
crying pollen tears
flitter through the
trustworthy void.

Moon

Moonlight bright white
night oasis
moon for the moon's sake
moon as a nightscape
the largest tear in the sky.

Nobody knows loneliness quite like the moon
destined to circle his love's sparkling eyes
unable to break the pull of her gaze
she mockingly drags him sky to sky
cosmos to eternity
and still back again

And so you stood there on a starry, clear eve
on a hill, on a plain of burnt prairie grass
dragging your train below veiled eyes
and when your arms spread out in a 'what??'
with a trained touch of the melodramatic
the full moon sat perfectly in the palm of your hand.
and me with too-few years of experience
to reference such travesty in one movement.

Untitled

I want to softly dress and
present you to the world
In something red and slinky
that amplifies your kitten purr

the purr of your morning side
sweet, fresh chocolate side.
Low with dread I'll bow
to the toothy accolades.

I want to shred your clothing to
reveal our dark obsessions.
Bind myself in the tattered fabric to
deify your feline ferocity
the ferocity of your mourning side
scarlet-clawed mewing side.

High with abandon I'll
hail my ravaged rind.

Pillory

On the day I turned forty
National Public Radio informed
Poles were immigrating
To Germany for work.

In youth my pole
Busied my hands in answering
Questions drawn from the bosom
Of a "happy to see you" aunt's embrace.
But she was only being Irish.
With years the novelty grows
Slowly to resignation; the longing
For the guilt of something, anything;
No longer a bright, new Christmas toy
But a habit; something to do.

Dresses then hid from us secrets
we never cared what was attached to.
Never satisfying the way a baby does (little did we know!)
We instead learn to notch memories with chance encounters
Of the closest we'll ever come to
Returning where we began.

You can never go home again
Hairs grows on and in the ears.
No one told me these things.
(You'd think there'd be a book)

There were fifty-two states
in geography lessons. I have
no clue where two of them have gone.
My only passing grade came there
when I was ten. I miss them.
Men are right about so few such things.
Or wrong, for that matter; life just
dries the skin in later years.
Sans oil, depleted by youth's flame,
The armor chaffs as acne dies;
between diaper rash and aged itches
there's a cup of cold, clean water.
Too quick warm, evaporate, die,
it soon rains back down
as coffee dregs and cigarettes.

I see my father in the mirror sometimes.
(there is no better place to hide.)
And mother-fuck him for my hairline
while hating him for really
being of the those.
(You can't love someone who did your mom.)

I don't care to know methods
of tuning a rough V-8
or to "shake it before putting it away."
(we only wipe our asses for woman's sake, anyhow)
I wish he'd have taught
how lonely love can be
and fickle; or warned
just where an angry prostate is found.
He never explained divorce lawyers
or bad knees. Children, too.

No parent should outlive their child.
God explained that by telling
Moses to lop the balls off Egypt.
Had I suspected I'd have painted
in blood the frame of the playpen
where she slept away this life.
She'd never resent my hairline, right?
Dresses can't keep secrets anymore, anyhow.

It's daunting, age's dawning
with the belly believing
the world really is a stage
as the toes cower in the wings.
They said red meat was poison once.
Now bread is the primary suspect.
I doubt crib deaths and car wrecks
care what we had for dinner.
All who ate Manna are dead now, too.

Grapes murdered you, and a show.
I hated you because I loved you;
jealous of your happy heart
because it was once mine,
when you opted to show another
thing attached to your secrets;
when you trusted your life to him,
but always took my keys;
when you doomed reconciliation,
and me to a new way of life:
recovery; painting blue my next ten years
entirely, making coping
my day's only purpose.
Still routing ravages though
mercenary dreams and counting
coups of miseries mine.

You should really be here for this part.
(That was the plan, remember?)
Having molted from my life
your butterfly drinks of
a different colored sky
leaving just an aging shell of me
where once lived her favorite toy;
a gift returned to the birthday boy
past the point of needing it.

Sunshine

Tossed on the morning with a sigh
She rises sluggish to her heights
just to dive in haste from steps on high
and in terror hide behind the night.

Just to be again heavenward hurled
to birth the dawn unnerving,
and shine upon a wayward world
which has yet to be deserving.

Etiquette's Long Faces

"One who pays attention to a statement is a
confederate of the speaker."

Plato

For Family Santiago: Felix, Paquite, & Veronica

And Dying

I knew that lightning might strike me today.
But did not a thing about it.

I foresaw the danger
Felt my hair stand on end.
Yet still stood I, and let it happen anyway.

What of this life that I've watched from afar
Like serenity from a thinking man
Or joy from the wise
How do I mourn that which I've never had?
Far be it from me to say.

As I knew the lightning might strike me today
But it's the sound of the thunder which I fear most anyway.

Tuesday

Writing is never easy
when thoughts roll off the mind
dissolving like an ebbing tide.

Where the seawater is bitter
tasting of dirty salt
microscopic plankton
rotting in your mouth like curses.

Still it reminds one of tears
with their own peculiar bitterness
when the heart rejects the mind's lead
and thoughts, like emotions, dissipate and drown

on paper and life.

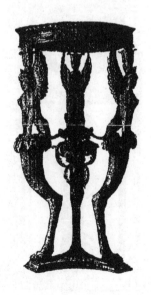

Watashiwa

My pen is now fading, though it is not refillable
Disposable, as they say.

So each word brings it nearer to death.
Closer to being thrown away.

Ever waiting is The Fall

The Victory

Sometimes when I am sad
I look far off, to the distant skies
And wonder if there doesn't exist
A parallel universe
Or another dimension
Where there are only good things happening
To ME
As compensation for all of this bad.

And might a careful wound carry me there

But then, with the light fading to infinity
I watch the razor's laughing glare
As if to say it has won
And this life was all that there is.

For Kevin

Star

Time is pressing and heavy
alive there's no reprieve
as I speed through each foggy day.

With night the mist clears
and in confined peace I'm alone
as I ponder my fated way.

Urgent, hostile dreams overtake me
till at a bright, cursed hour an alarm clock awakes me
and again off I race, Death's clock ticking faster
till I succumb to the sleep which as yet man can't master.

It rapidly fades away.

On A Bench In Omaha

Looking so ancient that her wrinkles
had sharp edges
like creases in the trousers
of a life-long soldier

there was a quiet poetry
in the smoke rings blown
by an old woman

those creviced eyelids full
in blink and smile
of the faint strains of a life-song.

Cliffs Of Vanity

I once had a cat, aged and mellow
With dazzling green eyes; fur soft and yellow.

He too had a comrade, a smallish gray mouse.
The two of them frequently stopped by my house.

Yet they'd never tarry
at any affair
But race back to the hovel
the two of them shared.

Secreted away far out back near the fence;
With seclusion afforded by foliage quite dense.

Absent from our world they had found peace of mind
In a cross-breed union, taboo to our kind.

Which explains their pure fight
when I uncovered them there.
As when they saw me coming
They knew such a scare

That the cat killed the mouse in their once-peaceful home
Then took his own life rather than be alone.

(or at least from the mouth of an odd ten year old
That is the story my mother was told

As she happened upon the carnage.)

For Lyin' Debbie

A New York Minute
On 9/14/01

alert eyes raised to the skies
no longer in hope, in reverence
in admiration, thanks, for a sunny, blue day

but scanning all directions in expectant anxiety
of disaster looming like a day star
shining down upon the masses
with evil intent.

Like a moue below blue skies
the cityscape wept.

Shadow Of A Doubt #1
Ride A Silver Swan

A portrait hangs upon my wall
a dreary one, of dark and all
Oh, how I wish that it would fall!
I want not that I be like him.

It seems at the same time moving and still,
and it serves the purpose yet invokes no thrill.
I am deemed soft, but desire to kill.
I want not that I be like him.

I want not that I be like him.

1/10

I awake in the dawn
to a warming sun
which caresses my face through the bars

West of the sunrise
I can still see the moon
wishing Good Day to the stars

While off in the distance
a slight wisp of smoke
reaches it's hand to the sky

And I wonder if it's fire
or wreckage, or war
and how many this time had to die

Then I wonder how I
could have slept so at peace
while people fall dead in the streets;

While our great leaders rant
about victims and loss
and "our" enemy's impending defeat.

Then I ponder an infant
straight away from the womb
knowing this world as he opens his eyes:

First he clenches his fist
– a last show of defiance
then he breathes, and then he cries.

III

Naked Crayons

"A little innocence creates a day."

e.e. cummings

For T.D., who knows why.
&
Sindy Karina Franco Sanchez
of Jumaya, Guatemala

Aide

Through squinting eyes, furrowed brow we peer
Sighing all the while
And recognize the bottomless depths
Of sadness and despair
Having pulled the milk cart
Below San Francisco suns
Right past beautiful, carefree souls.
Yet knowing full well a smile
Provides erasure of those lower, tougher doldrums
Should one be offered of a sudden
And like the fluttering wave of a fragile hand
Provide the impetus of a fossil fuel
To get we up that hill
With our own smile.

For Wheezie

The Lesson

———————

Tonight I danced naked
in the core of the city, on cold, heartless streets.
How ever did I come to be here?

I am vulnerable and exposed,
alone and quite misunderstood,
with my wilting, sallow flesh in view for all to see.
Strangely, I feel no shame.

I know no steps of fluid grace.
And, truth be known, am quite displaced
to lay one foot simply before the other.
Yet trod I onward, learning as I go.
I can see your incredulous stares,
as if you've cause to be surprised,
when in fact you never paid me any mind;
when I fact the dance goes on despised
by all who've ever walked these roads
but conveniently forgot that they had
once they knew the proper steps.

Do not mock my awkward steps,
nor scorn my errant strides.
For daily was I here beside you,
yet you taught me naught
nor did you try
to make more subtle the error in my steps.
You only cheered me on.

So today just smile at the dancing fool
as he passes *your* life by.

Inheritance

I wonder if I looked like me
one thousand lives ago
or wore the clothes, the skin, instead
of some other dimension's ego

and when someday this consciousness
again moves onward, upward, outward
I wonder what cloak awaits it
and if perhaps it might read these words
oh, ten lives hence
with a sense of heavy-heartedness
and wish it had written them.

Rib

Her curses danced upon and through me;
steel pellets of a shotgun blast
laying bare the sturdy rib
she resents descending from

passing out my other side
they pick up God, Adam, Elvis
and naturally Bukowski;
a web of male conspiracy.

Blaming us for childbirth
war, and the bikini
when she knows moon cycles
make her who she is.

Too, silly she, not seeing
it's one less bulkhead
for to stop her raging pain
upon our hearts.

For Joyce

Two

I wrote down love during spring repose
held its tail for the duration of a sigh
from end to end I adored it
till it loosed itself and fled

Like an autumn leaf's dying hues
it fades and yellows on the page before me
Oh, for a shredder, a match stick
or the nerve to rend it in two or more
millions
pour it upon the floor
then count the pieces;
dust in the sun

Once love lived for love's own sake
Not the death of which we might forsake.

To Listen

A still, small voice came calling through the darkness
with whispers of freedom and joy and revolt.

Silenced priests frocked in irons
struggled with conscience unequaled by lusts
and fought the good fight in scorn and defamation.

Of more than dust are we made; than death destined.
Yet a god's awakening passes not through doors
of desire framed in greed and ego

But lay dormant, flabby, slow
till such a time as that skeletal cry escapes us all
and a still, small voice can be heard.

For The Rev

Dobbin's Ferry

Once I was on towards Dobbin's Ferry
when approached an aged man.
When he smiled, so it seemed,
his ancient face beamed.
Then he offered his weathered, old hand.

"Why go ye," he asked of me,
"down this path so smoothly graveled?"
"For vines in seas, and knee-deep weeds
pave the road less-often traveled.

"And all my kin and friends before
have found wine and made merry
on this easily walked road," said I,
"which leads to Dobbin's Ferry."

"Ah yes." said he, rolled his eyes at me.
Then turned as if to go.
"Surely their footsteps are your path;
Their fates all that you'll know."

As he left the beaten path I stood
His words hard on my mind.
Then swiftly chased I after him
to see what I might find.

Perhaps my face will smile one day
and not look false or hollow.
And know then things I know not now.
And see if me they'll follow;
Away from Dobbin's Ferry.

A Special Place

There is a place I know of
where spring's always in the air.
Where loves grows carelessly at ease
because I know you're there.

It is a place where kisses fall
like raindrops from the sky
And we hug and kiss our son good-night
when sleep gets in his eyes.

It is a place not far away
Although we're far apart.
I go there when I close my eyes
and look inside my heart.

No judge can stop me being there.
No bars can keep me out.
No prison walls can hide the ones
that I can't live without.

While they might lock my body down
and cage my flesh in steel
They can not ensnare the love
that for you two I feel.

So as you dream of that special time
when they set my body free
Remember that place not far away
where you're always here with me.

Progeny

Headlong thrust
upon the yellowing pages of time
go the leagues of a searching generation
in a history all their own

The past calls them wayward;
directionless babes, doomed to fail
Xer's and Yer's, grungy dope fiends
sloth-like and lacking purpose, elan

Honor rests not in flowery graves though
nor wistful memories, fading newsreel
but in the eternal spirit of youth
and new blood spilled
in the inherent desire
to define themselves, find themselves, prove themselves;
write history uniquely their own.

The aged save memories; the young, worlds.
Tis the bold who carry the bright torch,
sprightly climb the high mountains,
even stair by stair
and like young lions romp
upon their fate, destiny, place
when honoring their call to arms
call to survive
call to *matter*
to their glory shall they go.

For the Saints of The Twins 9/11/01

Winter

A custard snow
gathers on a chipped-paint windowsill
waiting to be eaten
tasted/felt passing into
and through
being; a part of flesh
sour flesh
nourishing, cleansing
filling goodly
filtering impurities, smiling
passing out the other side
dirty slush on a city sidewalk.

Stalingrad, 1942

We were ordered to cling
to the Motherland bravely
I and my comrades
our back to the Don.

I, in artillery thunder
from which night would not save me
felt naked; empty rifle
frozen fast to my hands.

Yesterday's meal
was a cavalryman's stallion
tonight we eat snow
and still gnaw on our fear.

Friends' bodies lay strewn
on the ice of stilled river.
There's no wood for a fire;
even rats avoid here.

Hope too is frozen.
Dreams are a zephyr
blown across the wide canyon
of the passions of war.

I'd salute any flag
sing hard any anthem
for the sake of one quarter;
to hug my children once more.

The Climb

Two-by-two I race
sprinter – armed and lunging
up the tall spiral staircase
with the wide, eager grin
of a fortune's thief

till, sneaker on step / loafer on landing
I stop mid-stride at the last
bent, akimbo
sweat tears puddling on worn tiles
as I survey the view
of the cracked plaster walls of manhood
wondering of the journey's value
then grip tightly the railing
for the slow trek down.

L.R. Tears

Tears fall when Lou Reed sings,
"You can't always trust your mother."
Spewed by her once
to this samsaric circle
and squandering all the shapes, angles
of this rebirth
for ways back into that triangle
or any other;
the flesh prerogative
to destine my seed
to that same cruel betrayal.

IV

The Dove

"Everything hurts."

Michelangelo

*For Teresa, who was there once
but should not have been;
Who should probably be here now,
but is not.*

Women just don't get it sometimes.

Banner

You float like a note above me
having passed across the heart strings
a perfectly tuned vibration

An anthem that echoes through the soul
stirring the pride of a blind patriot
recurring
in the wisp of dreams.

I salute you.

Bronx Darling

For the third time in a very brief while
I met your eyes across a room
and wondered if you were stalking me
with some girlish brand of malevolence

till I realized, of a certain,
that I was, in fact, following you
with a uniquely boyish variety.

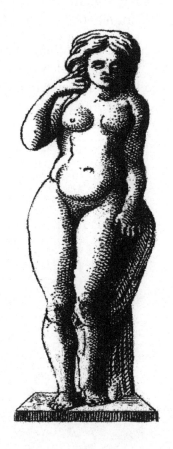

Eulogy

He never paced, never tramped
wearing out carpets, rugs,
but rather passed directly through life
with a small footprint
and large grin, smirk

Opting not to just sit there
till he didn't want to sit any longer
nor long enough to offer another
the opportunity to chase him off

Instead, he was one of those brilliant,
unassuming few
who learned the punch line
of life's etiquette
long before death
had a chance to track him down

For P-Bop

Clutch

I think of you at night
in that span of darkness, blooming,
and two times, three, I drift
to fade in that fantasy shade of gray;
sliding off Iike tired Velcro
towards the wailing keen of dreams
tho' find you there, too,
A clasped hand caught in a jar.

If I Could

If I could walk upon the moon
or caress the stars above
that would not sate my need for you
or make me less in love.

If I could bring all nations peace
and rid the world of war
my longing for you would still rage
and I'd only miss you more.

If I could climb the mountain high
or descend the canyon low
my desire for you would remain
No matter where I go.

So though I can not fly the skies
or swim the endless sea
In my heart I'm still a happy man
as long as you love me.

Journey

Lodestone aspirations
of a melancholy butterfly
lost in a sea of mountains
when raindrops smashed
instinct, of a better land,
stem-to-stern she plies
environs never quite noticed before
in abstract trepidation

Something To Call Your Own

You're afraid to hope, I can tell
and I know you don't belive in love anymore
and that this crazy life has left you feeling
quite alone and heroless.
But I'd like to try
– don't even ask why –
to put a song in your heart
and a gleam in your eye
and something true
like my love for you
into your heart so you'll believe in me
as I believe in you.
You've been through so very much bad in this life
and I've been there for so very little of it
that you find it hard to trust a man like me
– or any other man –
when all the others have wronged you so.
But cede the high ground, just one more time
allow yourself the hope of your youth
that you may indeed find one true love
with the winds of winter on a nearby wing
and closing ever faster.

Allow your heart to love again
lest life be bitter
and lonely remain
for all of your so-few days.

Let me shower you in the verbal trinkets
of affection that you long for
and dote on the special innuendos
two lovers share
in naughty touches
beneath tables in crowded restaurants
and not notice uncomfortable watchers
who wish us act our age.
Still, love Is for the young.
Of course the young at heart.
So do you always have to act so old?
And when will you ever let the smiles start?
When is the proper time
If ever there is one
To let yourself be loved?

Should I Lie

Should I say I didn't love you
It could only be a lie
I'm a flower in need of light and warmth
You're the sunshine in my sky.

Should I say I didn't miss you
That too would be untrue
With each beat of this burning heart
my soul cries out to you.

To say I didn't need you
Would be the biggest lie of all.
I'm a servant to your heart's desire;
I run each time you call.

Yet I could never lie to you
I cannot stories tell
The truth is my heart wears your love
And it fits me very well.

So should I say I did not love you
It must just be a lie
For I love you more each passing day
Than I did the day gone by.

Dressing

Sunshine rose before the alarm
with a smile parents long for

And H-I-J-K
CALEMENNO-P
she in singsong sang
kid-big ears parting pigtail wings
and holding aloft a precious grin
balanced perfectly
as she prepares to paint her day
with the array of bright colors, dreams
in her sock drawer
as if she'd spent the long, dark night
in watershed contemplation
and in her little girl musings discovered
a cookie.

Love Poem

I flip through dog-earred pages
back-and-forth across
times of my life
our life
the essence of you on every page
present as the unseen growth rings.

None seem special
meaningful anymore
just passé tributes
to dead, dusty love.
(What on earth was I thinking??
We'll never fuck like teens again!)
Some books bear closing
for the sake of pure closure.

A poem named passion
a passion named desperation
for being all we wanted
then being all we had
then being all we feared
and
so far
drawn into your dreams
I'd lay and watch time mark
it's passage across your eyelids
funny how I never saw emptiness coming
when
mesmerized by the sight
of soft milky skin behind your knees
I'd split the lonely darkness in reflection
of a rose alive in magma.

No bastardization
of movable type
earns passage over history
just by being there.
I can't write you out of my life
wite-out you out of my life
our history the skin
clinging to my frame;
these syllables written in
blood across the flesh of
a poor, dead tree
bring to life only
dreams of dead love.

Wahine

A wahine princess
dancing away a morning
one sun's trial, one moon's grief
to the song a rain drop sings
in a breeze so soft
you can hear the grass bow, then applaud
as Pele shudders aflame
with admiration, knowing
Heaven is the sand that
sails her sweat.

GoodBye In A Prison Visit Hall

Staring across the chasm
Which separates our two worlds
trapped by those crazy choices
which have brought us both here
I watched you watch me
watch you leave
stretching moments, just moments…
that's all there were, moments
until then there were no more.

My hands already missing
making love to your hands,
they trembled gently as
the elixir of mixed palm sweat
faded; they felt
as if the blood itself had flown
and suddenly the missing you returned
to escort me through those places where you're not.

You've perfected just that shape for me
I like to believe;
all angles, grooves, edges
blending, flowing into a seamless whisper
of heartbeats
in a therapy of form
a form of therapy
there must be an art to fitting so perfectly
within a fond embrace.
I've never felt anything so well there before,
never been hugged so thoroughly.

Your artistry is an island to me
in a sea of lost souls; I clung
with regret at having to stay even greater
than that sweet misery
of a rushed good-bye kiss
stolen in an unguarded moment
(We're all vampires of something, you know)
I wonder where that scar will hang his hat.
I think a treasure shines equally bright
be it stolen or otherwise.
I think sometimes it's worse to be restrained
than to risk those pains, those hurts, disappointments
that unrestrained openness threaten.
I think I ran too soon.

The poignancy of your beauty startled me.
Spring always catches me off guard.
(I can never think to remark on these things
once you've raped the sanctuary
of my dark brooding)
When you said I look the same
I was thinking you the sweetest candy
my eyes have ever tasted.

But then I shuddered at reading your shoulders
the shape, set of your delicate frame
when I spoke of being halfway, only.
(Even acting never hides everything)
You've been so patient with me, I know
all of this time; so true.
And I race against that place
where this is no longer a bargain for you.
(Which is not to say it ever was)
I'm slain by the thought:
I'll never get there in time.

So instead I merely cling
to the ghosts of days and visits past
hoping to wring the essence of you
from just one more of them, today
and I race, I race…

Caressed by your eyes, your smile
so many thoughts, emotions
dreams
leap to the surface
a world of observation waiting to be shared
but all lacking the opportunity
of an appropriate moment
all lacking a place, a proper place
in a place of only moments.
I suppose it's best to just keep my mouth shut
and dwell on banalities, where no hurts live
nor no risk of disappointing you.
Which all leaves me wading
through the cryptic symbolism
of letters, syllables, pencil leavings
trying to string together the passion, the joy
of having trusted you to someday return
and then being blessed for doing so.
(Always a good bargain in trusting you)

Yet the days still end in sadness
of losing you this day, and any other
or losing this day with you;
(the chance of stretched moments!)
And I know this life
this blinding flash of injustice
will never be enough of you for me
even if we live five hundred years
and that whatever lies beyond this
onward, upward, outward
owes me so very much more of you.

So at the chasm, there I stood
and made gassho, hoping you understood
that bow of reverence, of awe
for all that you do;
for all things you
and for the way that this scares me.
(and how maybe it scares you too)
My nerve ends genuflecting, a tingle in every finger
with the gratitude of exhaustion, or even usage
and unafraid to curtsy with the thrill
of just being awakened again.
Fish change color for the likes of that
and even birds have that plumage thing going on.
While I'm left with only muted shades of khaki brown
to puff-up and flaunt
but rainbow-hued songs of veneration and thanks
spill from a place I had thought outgrown
and I watch you watch me watch you
thinking these are the moments I live for.

So the mornings find me kissing the sun
then sending her along in the hope.
She'll too once catch you alone and unguarded
greet you so much better than I said good-bye
and then watch you watch her
dive into the
sea.

68 ❖

✦⟾ V ⟾✦

Myths & Legends

"To lie a little's not so bad
if it gets you
through the night"

Rod McKuen

For Art Bell, who should take himself more seriously

Of Church And State

The flair and prowess of the sot were imbibed illusions, which
only he could see. The clear, precise bars of an old pop favorite
which he heard passing oh-so-smoothly through his lips
were no more than boisterous, bad-breathed slurs to those
who happened by and were unfortunate enough to take notice
of him in their ears, their eyes, their nose, their zip code.
In fact, he was nearly a sensory overload.

He envisioned the sideways glances and repulsed scoffing
of the passers-by becoming a staring , standing awe as he
strutted past with glory in his eyes and greatness in his stride
– As if the casual observer were observant enough to observe
the casualties – as he made his way down the block.
(He was often called homeless, see, when in truth he felt
more at home among the current social dregs than he believed
possible were he to find himself in a land or time of lesser
greatness. He had fought for *his* country, you know.)

So he was left alone to sing and strut, step off the curb and
swagger his way into the angry face of rush hour traffic. Later,
as the fire department hosed his faced off of the pavement
and the line of vehicles began to move again, the story of his
bothersome demise was carried – *live via satellite* – into the
living rooms of America, as a footnote to a traffic jam report.

Later still, they called it a good day for the home team.

For Rudy Giuliani

Ab Ovo
(from the beginning)

I steer for the Pure Land
abstention from the void; the
benumbing detritus
of inculcated response which
would corrode the essential
I;
that mortality might be driven
down to it's sickly axles
burn the rubber from the rims
and leave it
to rust, dust, somewhere/along
that road in the sun
but to absorb only briefly
catch and release
to the cool of that Long Night
that the last warm spot
be the crown.

Once Upon A Time

———————

They were reunited by a former classmate exactly ten years past their brief High School fling. This time around they married after a whirlwind romance, and all their friends said it was great.

Fortunately, her womb was barren.

With a Niagara Falls honeymoon barely in their taillights, he accused her of cheating for the first time, which she truthfully denied. (She was, in fact, the perfect wife.) Shortly thereafter he turned possessive and mean, lost his job, and went bald, in no particular order. She remained petite, straw-haired, energetic, and a very hard worker. Friends thought her perky.

Opposites still attract in the land of Opportunists.

Thus she fed him, clothed him, and loved him, while he tried to subdue her vitality. He waited for her to return home from work every single day, and often beat her soundly if traffic held her up for five minutes. He questioned her faithfulness and devotion nightly, interrogating her till the wee hours of a work day's morning.
She gave up all of her friends and hobbies for *him*.
She tried to dress and smile for *him*.
She catered to his every need, walking on eggshells all the while. He abused her more and more.

So after ten *long* years of terror and abuse, she joined a battered woman's network that she'd heard about on TV, and left him forever.

She soon signed up for therapy, got a promotion at work, saved and bought a house of her own, reestablished old friendships, and for the most part moved on to better things.

He spent the rest of his life hating her for betraying him. (He had known from the beginning that she couldn't be trusted, see.)

And one fine, fine August evening after his dog died, with a sixpack in the fridge and the Mets up by three in the ninth, he killed himself to get back at her.

And she felt guilty for the rest of her life.

On The Wreckage

The older gentleman with the gray dime-store jacket and khaki trousers, pulled high above his navel, held the little boy's hand as they walked to the counter and sat down on the stools nearest the heater in an attempt to dry their shoes and chase the chill from their bones. After the waitress came over and took their order, the man mumbled a gruff, "Stay here, boy" and slipped away in the direction of the "Rest Room" sign, leaving the lad alone to busy himself by using the chrome ring around the base of the stool to scrape the mud from the bottom of his tennis shoes. When the man returned from the bathroom, half dragging his arthritic leg across the diner's linoleum floor, he had to stifle a moan of pain as he plopped his old bones onto the stool with a creak. As the waitress placed a plate holding a burger and fries in front of each of them a short time later, she couldn't help but notice the peculiar tone the man used to thank her, while the little boy just sat and stared. (She looked like someone's mom.)

After a few minutes, and only halfway through his burger, the child turned quickly and tugged at the old man's sleeve, pointed towards the window and shouted, "Look, G'amps! The rain is slowin' down!"

"Eat your burger, boy," was the man's brusque reply. But the boy kept staring at the door. He watched curiously as an elderly woman entered the diner, cursing the foul weather and shaking the raindrops from her coat with such vigor that her rosary beads jingled like a tired wind chime. The ruckus made the man look too, causing him to miss half of what the boy was saying, "...and you did say we could walk past the accident and have a look if the rain let up a bit."

"Boy, you're gonna' want my belt to let up on your ass if you don't eat that burger and be quiet!," G'amps said, as he turned back to his lunch.

"But G'amps," said the boy, "I betcha if we started walking now..."

"An' I betcha you'd better eat that damned burger!!," shouted the old man. The boy looked toward the swinging doors of the kitchen for the waitress, hoping for a motherly sort of person to argue his point to, but she was nowhere to be seen.

"Okay, boy," said G'amps after a few moments, "Okay, if that's how you want it." Then he stood up, cast an ominous smile down upon the lad, and snatched the half-eaten burger off of the little boy's plate, shoving it all into his own mouth at once.

And that's why, when the waitress walked up with the check, the old man's false teeth were making a clicking sound as he chewed, and the little boy was starting to cry.

Monday

I

The fish had gone all belly-up.
My favorite Oscar had X's in his eyes
like those on the sign
at the pond in City Park:
"No Fishing, No Swimming, No Boating," it said,
with little fishes underneath
with X's in their eyes.
I wanted to throw the smelly tank
across the dusty, quiet room
and bathe all these inanimate memories of you
in milky, stagnant water
and little colored rocks.
But you were not there
to fuel the anger in that way which only lovers can.
So hostile, raging thoughts waned
just as they had
when I threw your lamp down the stairs
and it shattered like the wall of anger
that had been holding back your tears
and you cried
then squinted and said,
"Ooh! You ASSHOLE!!" with a break in your voice
and I understood that you wanted
to kill me right then.
And that you loved me.

The radio was still on, barely audible.
But in a catchy ditty
heard I your name in a song.
Isn't it funny how these things happen?
I quickly pulled the plug.

II

I spoke your name one time aloud
just to see if it sounded the same here now.
but my voice was shaky as it echoed through rooms
left hollow by your departure
and rebounded off of loneliness so dense
that even the roaches seemed gone.
It made its way past me on the way out the window
where your favorite curtains once hung neatly.
But they were not there to hold it in.
The sound of it leaving was sad.

There was a partial roll of tissue
on the shelf near the door.
You probably left it there
while you carried something out to your car.
I can still see you clutching the roll
in your bare and child-like hand
as you sniffed and teared your way
from box to bag to bureau
packing trinkets and tissue-balls alike.
And I think you wrapped a few knick-knacks
and hoped
that anything broken during the move
could be mended when you arrived at your mother's.
Yet you suspected your heart was beyond mending.

III

As I wander the rooms
the bedroom beckons
like a strobe in a dark room flashing "Exit."
And I realized this room was our only connection
for such a long, long time
after communication moved away.
Not that we would have spoken any substance
since after love feels gone, words mean little anyway.
I notice you forgot your pillow. Sadness abounds.
I wonder if it smells as much of me to you
as it does of you to me
or if that is why you left it here
not knowing what it does to me.
Women just don't get it sometimes.
Your first night gone
I tried to sleep without it, and you.
Yet it's scent awakened me from afar
where I had tossed it angrily
in this abysmal darkness.
And grope though I had like a blind man
in this alien landscape called home
my own empty, dirty sheets are all I found.
I drift into the bathroom, but nothing's hanging there.
No drying hose today, nor frilly underwear.
That smell too has changed.
No longer the sweet, humid scent of you
but a medicinal, cosmetic aroma fills the air now
like an Italian grandma's nightstand
or the shaving kit of a sailor
on a sea borne submarine
months away from home
which washes upon the shore of a deserted isle
and finds me on the dunes. Alone.

IV

The telephone company
with all their incompetencies computerized
left the telephone on.
Just another passive torment.
I hold it in my hand queerly,
A rune of yesterday's ruins.
Words fail me.
There's a curious pulse in my throat
and my collar seems too damned tight
so I don't ring your mom's house
though I want to.
(I know I think I want to but I don't.)

I cannot bear to make myself dial
so I say hello to a dial tone.
Silly I, talking to a dead telephone.
It has betrayed me with the loneliness
it was created to repel. Imagine that!
Somewhere there are people
eating chocolate-chip cookies
and filling the air with vibrant, gay laughter.
And here I am talking to a dead telephone
with an errant tear streaking my cheek.
Wounded by the thorn.

V

Isn't this the way these things always happen?
How dreams seem to drift through your grasp
like a thread who's tail passes between your fingers
before you realize you've reached the end?
How love either fades
like the taste of strong wine on a lover's lips
or just fizzes out during the quiet times
and the morning shadows
in a jolt of reality
reveal that what's on your mattress
is as flat and as stale
as the warm can of beer left open on the nightstand
which seems so repulsive now?

So what if you accidentally
drop your love/roll it around
shake it up a little by mistake
and it explodes once opened
then in a defensive reaction
you shove it away from you
for fear of being sprayed?
How do you ever teach yourself
in such an untrusting land and time
to simply brush back the foam?

VI

I know it would have been worse for me
if you had been killed in a wreck
or simply died
and were ripped from my life
through no fault of mine.
Because then missing you
would mean that you're not happy either.
When at least today there's hope.
For you, at least. For you.

For me there's a peculiar sorrow awaiting
and I welcome it, in a way.
It has been my only true and constant friend,
and has never failed me on the darkest of nights,
since you went away.
I am embraced by it, without reservation.
Though it is suddenly still you that I long to hold.

VII

I guess it is time to be moving on now.
The road is calling and this is not home.
We took a wrong turn somewhere, I know
and, succumbing to pride
never asked for directions.

But the highway of life
is a toll road, we've proven
and the cost of a token is often extreme.
You always pay your own way, it seems
and the price is the same
if you rode with the top down
and the radio way up loud
singing
or rather impatiently searched for a rest stop
over the past fifty miles.
It's a subtly perilous journey.

I'm glad to have known and loved you, dear.
Glad too that the pain of failure
erases all airs.
I hate that it's taken this long for me
to be sorry for throwing your lamp down the stairs.

I pause at the door on my way out
looking back over my shoulder at the life we once lived.
I might shirk the good times.
But they're right, so I smile.

The Talk

I rest my chin on dirty hands
And ponder all tomorrow's.
and wonder where this dawning stands
in the time man only borrows.

But in writing of this tired world
– of wit and jizz and gloom –
I've seen selfishness is paramount
and near forever looms.

As does the saving grace of shame
in a drunkard's syllabus.
Intoxicated, we've soiled the earth.
How shall she soon soil us?

So light upon a shooting star
the withering imagination of youth.
And draw from it, from where we are
the visions of a future truth.

Or allow it drop upon the ground
and quench it's burning flame,
to inscribe unto the next one's birth
our children's charge of blame.

We can offer up a tissue now
for the fears those stars might cry.
Or just eat, drink, and be merry, friend,
and tomorrow let them too die.

Barfly

We were mired in clichés and fancies
and smiling like fish aground
to cover our soul's nakedness.

And we *lied*.

The drinks, the wet napkins, the lights;
None seemed enchanted
though quite possibly the night was; the lonely night.
I'm trying to recall your name
but today, as even then, it fails me.

I'm a master at practical solutions.
I lean to kiss your cheek
and cheap rouge and powder greet my lips
like guardians of the pores
hiding whatever is beneath
yet permitting bodily secretions
from without or within.

Boyishness abounds but I squash it.
One more sip and I'd have let you know
– One more ounce for a changed fate –
that today's clothes and deodorant do not hide
encounters from yesterday, nor those days before.
Yet fearing reprisals, I simply smile.

Even then I was a realist.
With dirty nails to probe
tar-stained teeth to grin behind
and construction worker's boots
I too was dressed to kill
– or be killed, it would seem –
and stoned into splendor.
You clearly fear reprisals as well.

I affect one who is moral.
And where has gone the satisfaction of a touch, ask I,
when a kiss is not but a kiss
but merely a prelude
to conversations on condoms and hang-ups?
To breach security we certainly lie.

We are all adventurers, born to discover;
explorers one and all.
As lights flash and sirens wail in the dark night
– the dark, lonely night –
it is No No No
and then Well No, Maybe.
Wanting to believe, we trust
the satin fabric of fantasy
to caress away our fears.

An embrace is rough and rude on the street corner
and impatient. Embarrassed
we wipe our mouths and walk off together
silent and, yes, concerned, but not alone.
I think you had one of those flower names.
I think it sounded pure and clean.
I think we always lie.

We are all only memories waiting.
Now I've got to go, got to go
for I'm dying to make mine happen.
There's a dark, dark box being built for me somewhere
and this sad doctor's treatments
are just another fitting for it.
Though one size seems universal
and there's comfort in none.
My mirrored image appears aware of that.
The doctor asks if I think you knew.
I say by now I'm sure you do.
I wish I remembered your name.

For the Quilt's voices

Turnstiles

Subway turnstiles
open a place for us;
the spread legs
of a greedy paramour;
perhaps too a trebuchet
launching us towards Fate.
Destiny the cost of a token
and maybe a stale Marlboro
tossed to an idle homeless gal
who opts to toss it back
repeatedly.

I

It is I, It is I;
who you feel watching
in an empty morning kitchen;
on your lonely road.
I who tickles
the soles of your feet
through nightlife heels;
under bedtime sheets.

It is I who rings queerly
your quiet room ears.
It is I, the unseen movement
in the mirror beyond your eyes.

It is I, the hostile sunshine
piercing early morning dreams;
that unformed question
frozen at your parted lips;
It is I.

Spin

Revolving doors turn inward
fully half the time
yet still tether the outbound

Justice is a metaphor

sight never cures all blindness
when only dark shadows
tickle hairs backing the iris
A million broken-bottle sidewalks
run from diaper to D-block
where even the roaches chain smoke
and tote shanks
a soul-token toll road.

Torque

Times torn from a part of you
tastes, sounds I've missed of you
in life's busy, carefree hours.

There are places you just don't know
inside of you
long I've burned to set
my hands upon them hotly.
Wiling away a day's battle of thought
– the truth too boring to be believable –
I'd hide from you, hide with you
hide in you, burrowed
into that safe haven
God knows just how far down
with damp towels, sweaty t-shirts on stand-by
to wipe away the dregs of our fear
as
fretting again that damned unmade bed
we danced.

Our world a place I never understood
in your hand lay truths for me
of all expected of me
of all there ever was for me
I go there behind my eyelids still
or search again palm creases for
that place you liked best.

Every seed lusts soil and sun
earth and heaven.
Grand entrances present themselves
a blossom at a time
too, debutante daisies
traversing the long, red carpet
walk on eggshells in high heels
yet fear no awkward motions.

You bide time for fear of blooming
cracking shells or stumbling
and not trusting me to grasp you with
the aged, strong, scarred
hands of a grandfather
you root to stone, that careless gusts
not sweep away bits of carefree chaff
while the wind is simply content
to wrap around you in passing.

A quiet breeze blows
through the portals of a still night's
me
and the tastes, sounds I've missed of you
in life's busy, connected hours.

Chimera

"You have ravished me away
by a power I cannot resist."

John Keats

Whimsy

Whimsical dreams of
date palms and dharma texts
ride the wisps of heat aloft
o'er a stoic soldier
who, ajoy, in his cups,
holds dear honor to
the roof of his mouth;
a flagon's dregs left perennial
the backwash of cowardice
when, from somnolent history
he'd shock to find
nothing's changed sans the need
of time enough to die in.

Child

Youth is such a fleeting sin.
Dare I share mine with you?
So that the shifting truths of a child's memory
Are referenced in your heart, too?

Or that a smile's warm and knowing eyes
Are perceived by you as well,
When a friendship's joys and sorrows
Alone remain to tell?

Will you tell me of tomorrow?

Galleria

Steel-mouthed maidens
promenade about the shopping mall
just longing to be wooed
subdued
warmly, softly cooed to
the hearts of Americana
on display/on sale
with pizza and lawnmowers
Japanese electronic wizardry
and ad space.
The heartland cries in the loneliness
of postpartum adulthood
and acne.

In The City

In the Sunday morning city
slumbering bells yet to chime
grotesque tickles to our guilt's fancy
there's still no virgin place
my foot might touch.

Soles interrogating the quiet
in a skirmish of pavement and patent leather
my hips exaggerate the motion
while motion gives no quarter
refusing to be heeled
on such a crowdless day.

Bleed

The skinny guy with the lipstick smile
plays piano like it's a cheap, fat whore;
melancholy floats upon a cloud of cigarette fumes
while you've picked the label from your
genie-in-a-bottle
one nailful at a time
as if tearing the scabs away
from one heart's burns
might allow the pain
to bleed out.

Tort

———❧———

An Indian Summer smile
where October procrastinated
till the tourists went home
and the raked leaves sat
in mouldering piles
pissed at being victims;
cheated.

Leak

———❧———

A deceptive sadness drips
from the open wound of her eyes
animal magnetism
sucking steely-strong pity from his pores
leaves only a spineless mass
of boy pulp.

Rosa

―――◦◦◦―――

Rider sits in front
Siege Perilous to black men
Rosa's Holy Grail

Summer Haiku

―――◦◦◦―――

Blue gas attendant
summer bright smile girl passes
heart grows noble seed

Dawn Haiku

―――◦◦◦―――

horizon's dawning
a rust-red blanket sunshine
shadows bleed away

Haiku 747

streetlight glows brightly
moth stalks in the dark of night
the moon hangs laughing

Moon Haiku

passionless full moon
penetrates smoky night clouds
a faked orgasm

Hip Fish

river reflects trees
trout bursts through branches/hangs/falls
slaps fins with his pals

Made in the USA
Coppell, TX
18 February 2021